PERFECT **RECALL**

Increase your confidence,learn faster,
be more productive, & be memorable.

Edition 0

ISBN-13: 978-0-9823708-4-1
ISBN-10: 0-9823708-4-9

[   ] Like A Mind Reader

Contents

PREFACE

I intend you to *use* this book.

Don't be afraid to write in it. Take notes. Scribble.
Draw. Highlight. Dog ear pages.

Whatever it takes for you to put this information
into practice; do it!

People say knowledge is power, but knowledge does
nothing for you if you don't **use** it.

INTRODUCTION

How many times have you been introduced to someone and their name immediately evaporates? Ever torn up your living room looking for your keys? Forget your sweetie's birthday? Want to spend less time studying? Been at the grocery store, your phone dies, and now you have no clue what's on your list? Learning to play a new instrument or other skill?

Want to: Improve your relationships? Your business? Your studying habits? Make people feel important? Get better at public speaking? Reduce your dependence on your smartphone?

If you said yes to any of these, then this book is for you.

If you said no, you're not human.

YOU GOTTA WANT IT

How many times have you heard someone say, "I forgot. . .?" Probably more times than you can count.

The thing is, most people who say "I forgot" never even remembered what they were supposed to not forget in the first place!

A fundamental principle of any memory system is Initial Awareness. You, first, have to be aware of whatever you want to remember if you're going to remember it. Most people don't want to remember something, so they don't even bother being aware of it.

All the systems we will cover in this book work on the simple principle of focusing your mind on something long enough to kick-start Initial Awareness.

A concrete example: How bad are you with names? "I can never remember anyone's name! It's like they say it, and it immediately evaporates like I never heard it in the first place!"

A lot of times, you don't hear it! You're too busy thinking about how you look, what you're going to say, telling yourself you're not going to remember their name, etc. You're thinking about everything but remembering their name. Another point; you think you'll never see this person again, so you don't need to bother remembering their name.

Here's how you can help yourself out.

Next time you're introduced to someone, focus solely on hearing their name. If you don't hear it the first time, don't feel bad if you have to say, "I'm sorry, I didn't catch that right, could you repeat your name for me?"

The person will be flattered you're not just glossing over the introduction. You're showing active interest in the other person, and that goes a long way to endearing yourself.

Now that you've actually heard the name, use it a couple times in the course of the conversation. This creates a couple experiential anchors for the name to stick to. Instead of just thinking of their name, you've said it aloud which incorporates another sensory link to the name.

All the systems we'll be covering will slow you down

just enough to make you initially aware of whatever it is you want to remember. It might seem clunky & convoluted at first glance, but the more you use the systems, the more you'll remember, and the more smoothly integrated the system will become in your everyday life.

Soon, it will be second nature to have **PERFECT RE-CALL.**

JONATHAN **PRITCHARD**

INTAKE EVALUATION

Before you get into the details on improving your memory, it is useful to get a sense for how well your memory is working, now, before any enhancements.

Note: DO NOT SKIP THIS! It's easy to think, "He's not talking to me. I'm one of the cool kids who doesn't need to take tests." If you don't actually do this, you won't have empirical data **proving** you got better. Without that result, your gains will feel... meh.

Here we go.

Get a pen and the timer on your phone. Set it for 2 minutes. In just a moment you're going to start the timer, turn the page, and you'll see a list of 20 items.

Commit as many of those items to memory in that 2 minutes, and when the timer is up, turn the page again.

Ready? GO!

The List

- Banana
- Picture Frame
- Cat
- Lightning Bolt
- Post-It Note
- Mercury
- Skateboard
- Candle
- Dime
- Power Strip
- Movie Ticket
- Pencil
- Poker Chip
- Stool
- Guitar
- Baseball Cap
- Stop Sign
- Wind Chimes
- Brush
- Newspaper

Remember: At the end of 2 minutes, turn the page.

Now wait for 30 seconds before trying to write down as many as you can remember:

01.	11.
02.	12.
03.	13.
04.	14.
05.	15.
06.	16.
07.	17.
08.	18.
09.	19.
10.	20.

How did you do?

Due to the principles of primacy and recency, you should remember the first couple items on the list, and the last couple.

The ones in the middle are usually the more difficult items to remember. Now you know how good (or bad) your memory is!

WHAT IS MEMORY?

A useful model I use to think about memory is a web-like net of associations. When you think of one thing or idea, you automatically think about several other things that are connected to the first idea.

Every one of those associations automatically brings up a whole new cloud of associations.

This creates a web of connections created from the information in your mind. The more connections between pieces of information you have, the stronger your web.

If you're trying to learn something new, and it is associated with things already stored in your web, it gets caught in your memory more easily than a random factoid.

For example, if you think of the word "baker" you automatically bring to mind bread, the smell of a bakery, rolls, white shirt, flour, etc.

There are tons of connections linking the word "baker" to other details.

When you meet someone named Baker, however, you may not know anyone else named Baker, so the web of associations is non-existent, and the name has nothing to stick to.

As quickly as you hear it, the name escapes you.

That's why you can remember the word baker easily, and forget the name Baker even easier.

Since you remember something new if it is associated to something you already remember, the challenge, then, is how to create a web that will automatically link any new piece of information you're trying to remember.

That is what this book aims to do. By the end you'll have webs in place for names, faces, words, numbers, details, or anything else you want to remember.

I use the very same techniques in this book to amaze

audiences across the world. I'm sure you'll find it incredibly useful in all areas of your life.

Use your new powers for good!

HISTORY OF MEMORY

The earliest system used to improve memory dates back to a Greek man named Simonides of Ceos who lived around 556 – 468 BCE.

As the story goes, this guy was at a dinner party. He gets a call from a buddy, and he goes outside to get better reception.

While he's outside, the banquet hall collapses killing everyone inside. The wreckage made identifying the bodies impossible, but Simonides realized he could identify each person was based on remembering where they were sitting at the table.

This realization created the field of Mnemonics: the use of simple systems to improve memory recall, named after the Greek Goddess of Memory, Mnemosene.

The system Simonides was using is called "**Loci**" and remains one of the most pervasive memory systems still in use today.

Also called a "**Memory Palace**' it involves taking an imaginary tour through a large house, or building with many rooms. The more cubbies, alcoves, & details the better. As you walk through, you place mnemonic images in different areas in the palace.

Now, to remember something, all you have to do is walk through the Palace in your mind, and look at all the imagery you placed there.

When you see each mnemonic representation, you'll be remember what it means and voila! You have just remembered something!

For example, you could use the home you grew up in, your favorite apartment, or a museum you know inside-out. Whatever Palace you choose, the process remains the same.

Move from the front to the back of the Palace, placing the items you want to remember in each room. As you walk back through the Palace, each item will be waiting for you.

www.likeamindreader.com

Try it now with the following list of items: ball, vase, glass, gun, stuffed bear, cell phone, monkey, & map.

I'll wait while you put each item in your Palace.

Retrace your path through the Palace, and see what's in each room.

How did you do? Surprising how simple but effective it is isn't it?!

Once you understand the basic principle, you aren't limited to buildings and places.

If you're a mechanic, you can use a car. Start at the front, and work your way back: bumper, headlights, engine, windshield, dashboard, driver's seat, passenger seat, back seat, trunk, back bumper, and wheels.

This gives you 11 places to link items. If you're more familiar with cars than I am, I'm sure you can create a lot more places to associate details.

Use whatever is familiar to you, and always take the

same path through the image. You could even use your own body!

Start at your toes, feet, ankles, shins, knees, thighs, belly button, chest, neck, and head.

Instead of each body part, image they're whatever you need to pick up at the story. Your toes are now broccoli, your feet are eggs, etc.

It's incredible how simple it is when you know what you're doing.

There have been many improvements to the Greek's simple Method of Loci, and I will take you on a tour of the most popular & useful systems of Linking, Pegs, and Phonetic Alphabets.

ACRONYM SYSTEM

The Acronym System is very basic. The first letter of each word in a saying will match the first letter of the items you want to remember. Many people's first exposure to this system is in school when trying to remember the order of planets.

Planets of Our Solar System: Mercury, Venus, Earth, Mars, Jupiter, Saturn, Uranus, Neptune.
My Very Eager Mother Just
Served Us Nine Pickles

Colors of the Spectrum: Red, Orange, Yellow, Green, Blue, Indigo, Violet
The name: Roy, G. Biv

Scale of Mineral Hardness: Talc, Gypsum, Calcite, Fluorite, Apatite, Orthoclase-Feldspar, Quartz, Topaz, Corundum, Diamond
Tall Girls Can Flirt And Often Find
Questions That Can Dazzle

Great Lakes (East to West): Ontario, Erie, Huron, Michigan, Superior
Old **E**lephants **H**ave **M**uch **S**kin.

Order of geological time periods: Cambrian, Ordovician, Silurian, Devonian, Carboniferous, Permian, Triassic, Jurassic, Cretaceous, Paleocene, Eocene, Oligocene, Miocene, Pliocene, Pleistocene, Recent.
Camels **O**ften **S**it **D**own **C**arefully. **P**erhaps **T**heir **J**oints **C**reak? **P**ersistent **E**arly **O**iling **M**ight **P**revent **P**ainful **R**heumatism

How many days in a month? Some people remember the rhyme:

"Thirty days have September, / April, June, and November. / All the rest have 31, / Except February alone, / And that has 28 days clear, / And 29 in a leap year."

I prefer a visual association to remember them. With this, you recite the months in order, and the months that fall on a knuckle have 31. The months between the knuckles have 30 (except February).

Metric System: Kilometer, Hectometer, Dekameter, Meter, Decimeter, Centimeter, Millimeter

King **H**enry **D**ied **M**onday
Drinking **C**hocolate **M**ilk

There are many other pieces of information you can remember with acronyms! Be adventurous and make your own!

LINKING

Linking is a basic, yet powerful, skill that is the process of creating wild, vivid, and peculiar mental pictures that are associated with each other. We've already touched on what it is since every mnemonic system leverages Linking, but this system will focus on using Linking exclusively.

The main drawback to Linking is, it only allows you remember the particular sequence of items and not the position of any one item. It is perfect, however, for remembering a list of items you need to buy at the store, the topics you would like to cover in a speech, or the errands you need to complete today.

Maybe you need to get your haircut, buy staples, get chicken for dinner, write a letter to a friend, and book tickets for an upcoming trip. To remember these tasks, Linking would work perfectly. In order to use Linking, boil down each task to a single word that represents the whole task. Use words that you can easily visualize.

Now we start.

Say you want to start your errands after breakfast, so we link the first item to your breakfast routine. This way, as you go about your day, you will automatically come across the reminder for the first item on your memory list.

Imagine the following:

There's a bunch of hair in your cereal bowl.
Hair is stapled to a chicken.
A chicken is writing a letter.
The letter is folded into an airplane.

In most cases you will have to create an image between each pair of items. Here, we managed to get it down to four since we combined the hair, staples, and chicken together.

You can see how effective this process can be! The more outrageous you make the associations, the easier you will recall them when they are needed. Normal narratives are too plain, and do not create the indelible mark on your imagination that you truly need for long term recall.

Some other tips for improving recall:

- Make an item absolutely ridiculous
- Play with proportion (Make it too big or too small)
- Make it sexual (nobody has to know what you're doing.)
- Substitute (Instead of using a brush, you're coming your hair with a turkey leg.)
- Make it funny
- Exaggerate quantities (Instead of one item, imagine a whole rain shower of them)
- Put yourself into the scene. See yourself actually using an object, or doing an action

Use as many of these principles on this list as possible. Now let's say, for some reason, you want to memorize a list of random items. How would you go about it?

Well, when memorizing a list, it is not important that you memorize the exact order of the items. It is important, however, you do not forget any items. How would you know if you forgot an item if you didn't know the order? One way to accomplish this is to use the linking system.

Here is the same list from earlier:

Banana, Picture Frame, Cat, Lightning Bolt, Post It Note, Mercury, Skateboard, Candle, Dime, Power Strip, Movie Ticket, Pencil, Poker Chip, Stool, Guitar, Baseball Cap, Stop Sign, Wind Chimes, Brush, Newspaper

Let's use linking to improve your ability to recall them!

The first object on the list is "**Banana**." Imagine a guy inside a banana suit who is only a foot tall. If you need to close your eyes to imagine that as clearly as possible, take a moment to do so.

Banana to Picture Frame

The next step is to associate the first object, "Banana" with the next object, "Picture Frame." Imagine a picture frame around a picture of someone you know, but the frame is made of bananas which are growing brown, moldy, and have juice running all over the table. Once you have the image in mind, forget it and move on.

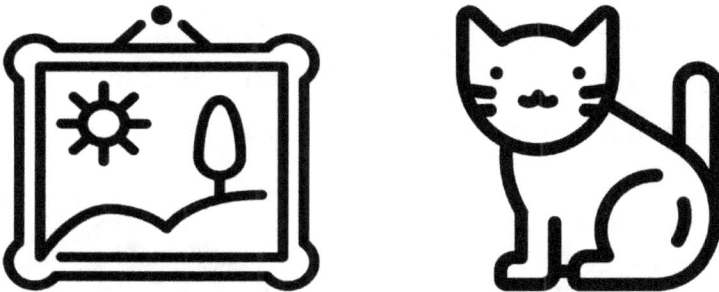

Picture Frame to Cat

The most recent thing you have associated is a picture frame, and now you will link it with the next object,

39

"Cat." I think of a cat crafting a picture frame from endangered wood. If you have a cat, you can think of that one, or Tony the Tiger from Frosted Flakes will do. Whatever comes to mind first is usually the best option. Don't spend too much time trying to come up with the craziest picture you can. Usually the first one is good enough.

Cat to Lightning Bolt

Let's continue through the items. Tony the Tiger bends over showing his backside, and you can see the tattoo of a lightning bolt on his backside.

Lightning Bolt to Post-It Notes

As you reach for the eye-bleach from Tony's tattoo, lightning flashes and Post-It Notes rain down from the sky; completely obscuring everything else.

Post-It Notes to Mercury

You can imagine a Mercury brand car made entirely from Post-It Notes, or you can write on Post-It Notes which are car sized.

Mercury to Skateboard

This one is easy for me because I grew up reading comic books, and I always enjoyed Silver Surfer. His surfboard is shiny just like mercury, and I substitute his surfboard with a skateboard. If you can link mercury and skateboard in a different way, do it!

Skateboard to Candle

While you skate down an almost vertical incline, your board starts to melt away like a candle causing you to wreck in a spectacular and painful way. Really picture yourself getting hurt badly and you won't forget it.

Candle to Dimes

You have a friend who found candles that, when lit, changes the wax into dimes. Their apartment is filling to the ceiling with dimes and the floors are creaking from all the weight.

Dime to Power Strip

Another easy one for me, as I can remember putting metal objects in power outlets. Really try to picture what it feels like to be electrocuted by the outlet.

Power Strip to Movie Ticket

At a theater you are handed a person sized power strip, rather than a ticket.

Movie Ticket to Pencil

Don't imagine writing on a ticket with a pencil, as that is too logical. You have to make it as insane as possible. Picture being overcharged for your ticket and you stab the attendant with a pencil.

Pencil to Poker Chip

You show up to an exam naked with only a poker chip to write with.

Poker Chip to Stool

You are in Vegas and you've just lost your last poker chip, so you destroy the machine with your stool. Try to imagine how it sounds as the metal and wires break apart and fly everywhere. Are people screaming at the outburst? Make it real in your mind.

Stool to Guitar

Each leg of the stool is a fully functional guitar, and you're playing in front of 100,000 fans who are screaming your name. You're the only person in the world who can play a 4 guitar stool.

Guitar to Baseball Cap

You're trying to play a guitar that is as tall as a building, and you are using your baseball hat as a pick.

Cap to Stop Sign

Your baseball cap is covering a stop sign which causes an incredible multiple car accident. Several people need to be hospitalized.

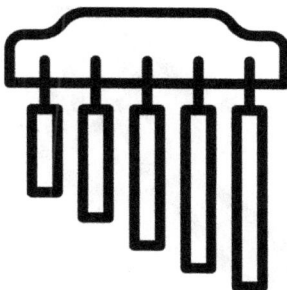

Stop Sign to Wind Chimes

A huge set of wind chimes made from stop signs hangs mere centimeters above your nose as you try to sleep.

Wind Chimes to Brush

The sound of wind chimes annoys you so much you use your hairbrush to destroy them. Really picture yourself going medieval on them!

Brush to Newspaper

You look in your hair brush, and it looks like it is absolutely full of dandruff, but instead it is finely shredded newspapers.

That's it!

All you have to do to remember the whole list is think of the first item, "Banana." That will call to mind the banana picture frame, which will immediately start the cascade of associated images.

Whether you start at the beginning and go forwards, or start at the end and go backwards, it will not matter. You'll be able to recall each item in the proper order.

SPEECHES

Many people rely on note cards, powerpoint slides, or worse yet fully written speeches when speaking to a group. Never again will you need to rely on a crutch while giving a presentation.

By using linking, you will be able to remember every detail you want to share with your audience. This works best for topics you know well, but you just want to make sure you don't leave out any details.

To do this, break the details you want to cover down to a list of bullet points. Then, take the bullet points and link them together.

Once you start your speech, you recall the first detail and say what you want to say about it, and then move on to the next detail prompted by the link you created earlier. Now you are a speech giving super star!

PERFECT **RECALL**

PEG SYSTEMS

You now know how to memorize long lists of items using Linking. What happens, then if you forget one of the links? You forget everything that comes after it. Also, what if you wanted to recall what the 8th item in the list is? You would have to start at 1 and count your way in. This becomes especially troublesome for long lists.

I like to think of Linking as a bunch of coats stuffed one inside the other. If you want to get to the 8th one, you have to remove the first, the second, and then the third, and so on until you get to the one you want.

Here, we will explore the power of Peg Systems. Instead of stuffing coats inside other coats, think of Peg Systems as hooks on the wall where you can hang the coats on the wall. If you want a specific coat, you can grab it off the wall without disturbing the others. The Pegs will give you a solid anchor to "hang/link" new information on.

This allows you to memorize lists in and out of order.

There are many Peg Systems. We already touched on a couple, though you didn't know that's what they were called. The Memory Palace is a type of Peg System. The Body Anchor system is a Peg System. The Automobile is a Peg System.

VISUAL PEG SYSTEM

This system relies on thinking of an object that resembles that number.

1. Match Stick
2. Swan
3. Heart
4. Sail
5. Hook
6. Golf Club
7. Cliff
8. Hourglass
9. Flag
10. Bert and Ernie (A skinny guy, and a round guy)

You can see how each item resembles the number it is associated with. Now, to memorize a new item, you would link it to the image associated with the number. For example, in the list of 20 items from earlier, the first image is a banana. You could think of striking a banana on a matchbox and it bursting into flames. The second would be a swan with its neck wrapped around a picture like a photo frame. The third could be a cat using your heart as a scratching post until it is completely shredded.

Note: Use your own imagery if it makes more sense to you. Instead of a match, you might think a candle would fit better. Great! Do that! Whatever you decide on, never change it. The pegs stay the same across time, and it's the newly associated details that change.

RHYMING WORDS

This is one of the most common Peg Systems, and if you learn best by hearing, this might be the one you like the most. If this is as far as you expect to go in training your memory, ok, but if you decide you want to extend your systems, I would advise you not to lock this one into your everyday practice. It may cause you confusion when you begin working on the Major System when we cover the Phonetic Alphabet.

The Rhyming Peg System is similar to the Visual Peg System, except you use words that rhyme with each number.

1. Gun
2. Shoe
3. Tree
4. Door
5. Hive
6. Tricks
7. Heaven
8. Gate
9. Wine
10. Hen

Here you would imagine being in a shootout firing a banana. There's a shoe on your desk with a picture in it.

There's a giant tiger stranded in a tree. And so on.

PHONETIC ALPHABET

The earliest European reference to memorizing numbers by turning them into words was given by the French mathematician Pierre Hérigone in his book Cursus Mathematicus, published in Paris in 1634.

This process has been known by many names, and many incarnations.

To make it easy, I'll be sharing the version I learned.

At first, it may seem confusing, and like more work than it would take to just remember this stuff with brute force. Once you practice with it for awhile, it will become second nature, and you'll fully realize how powerful this technique truly is.

This system is called the Phonetic Alphabet because you convert 0-9 into phonetic letters. Then, you take the letters and create words from them.

As a result you will find you can use the linking system - combined with this alphabet - to learn lists and numbers reaching into the millions.

Do you think you could remember the number:

**92297148437151229519011213474
0719417215139401493817192059746
9015714909579019022163094620994**

It's easier than you might think.

THE CODE

Here is the simple breakdown of numbers and how
they translate to the Phonetic Alphabet. Learn it.

1.	= t, d	6.	= sh, ch
2.	= n	7.	= K, hard "C"
3.	= m	8.	= V, F
4.	= r	9.	= B, P
5.	= L	10.	= Z, S, C

Now some of these associations might be a little difficult to remember at first, but once you think about it,
it is not all that hard to remember that fou**r** ends in an
R, and the Roman numeral 50 is an L.

You will quickly realize that once you have one letter
associated with its corresponding number, it is rela-
tively easy to remember the other letters associated
with it. This is due to the sounds of the letters being
similar.

For instance, S sounds like Z in when spoken in a
word so both S and Z represent Zero. T, D, and TH
all sound similar. As for the soft g and hard g, a soft g
as in "George" sounds like a J. The hard G as in "Ga-
rage" sounds like a K.

Vowels and other letters such as H are ignored if they
are not on the list. They mean nothing unless they
sound like the phonetic alphabet letters.

Using this system we can quickly see that any word
can be turned into a number. For instance, the name
Tom becomes the number 13 (t=1, m=3).

Or the word **PaRa-GLiDeR** can be turned into the numbers 947514 (p=9, r=4, g=7, L=5, d=1, r=4).

The reverse can be done as well, for instance 13 can be turned into the word **DiMe**.

You can see how you could make up peg words as you went along, but if you learn a series of peg words that you use all the time for this Phonetic Alphabet you will find a whole new world opens up to you.

Here are the numbers one through ten. Memorize these words:

1. ha**T**
2. he**N**
3. **M**a
4. hai**R**
5. ow**L**
6. **SH**oe
7. **C**ow
8. hi**V**e
9. **P**ea
10. **T**oe**S**

Once you have these committed to memory, it will be easy to recall the peg items. As soon as you think of 7, you will think of the K sound, which will tell you it is a Cow.

As with the Peg System earlier, it is easy to remember a list of ten items - but not only will you remember **what** the items are, but you will recall *where* they are, too.

For example, say you wanted to remember the following list:

Cellphone, Fork, Keyboard, Coaster, Backpack, Table, Cup, Shirt, Nail Clipper, and Statue.

We might make the following links:

1. Giant cellphone wearing a hat.
2. A hen using a fork to pole vault.
3. Your Ma typing on a keyboard with one finger.
4. A man's hair (toupee) being blown away on a coaster.
5. An owl hiking in the city with a backpack.

6. Using your shoe as a table to eat lunch off of.
7. Cow drinking coffee from a cup.
8. Wearing a bee hive as a shirt.
9. Using the nail clipper to take off peas from your nails.
10. Carving a statue using only your toes.

Now, if I asked you what was at number 7, you would think of a cow, and then think of the image of the cow drinking coffee from a cup.

If I asked you what is at number 3, you'd think of your Ma, who is slowly typing away at a keyboard.

You don't have to stop at a list of 10 anchor words for this peg system. You can go with as many as you'd like.

100 is a good start, and will serve you for most occasions. Insert words that match the Phonetic Alphabet, yet are easy for you to remember.

For example, if you prefer to think of a Tie for number 1, instead of a haT, that's fine. Whatever you choose, stick with it. Never change it again.

60

This becomes your master system that will always be with you, ready to work for you!

Here is the rest of the list for you to get started. Remember, make them visually engaging, controversial, violent, exciting, or otherwise interesting.

11. **TaT**: a man tattooed from head to toe
12. **TiN**: an empty tin can
13. **DaM**: a huge natural dam
14. **TiRe**: a huge tractor tire
15. **ToweL**: snapping a towel and hitting the object
16. **DiSH**: your favorite dish or serving platter
17. **DuCK**: a horse sized duck
18. **DoVe**: my Mom's favorite chocolate
19. **TaPe**: being duct taped to the wall
20. **NoSe**: that thing on your face

The numbers 21-100 continue on the next page.

21. Net
22. Nun
23. Gnome
24. Nero
25. Nail
26. Notch
27. Neck
28. Knife
29. Knob
30. Mouse
31. Mat
32. Moon
33. Mime
34. Mower
35. Mole
36. Match
37. Mug
38. Movie
39. Map
40. Rose
41. Rat
42. Rain
43. Ram
44. Roar
45. Reel
46. Rash
47. Rock
48. Roof
49. Rope
50. Lace
51. Lad
52. Lane
53. Lamb
54. Lair
55. Lilly
56. Leech
57. Leg
58. Loaf
59. Lip
60. Cheese
61. Sheet
62. Chain
63. Jam
64. Jar
65. Jail
66. Judge
67. Chick
68. Chef
69. Ship
70. Case
71. Cat
72. Coin
73. Comb
74. Car
75. Coal
76. Cash
77. Cake
78. Cave
79. Cab
80. Vase
81. Fat
82. Phone
83. Foam
84. Fire
85. File
86. Fish
87. Fog
88. Thief
89. Fob
90. Bus
91. Bat
92. Bone
93. Bomb
94. Bar
95. Ball
96. Beach
97. Pig
98. Puff
99. Pope
100. Daisies

And those are all the anchor words for items 21 through 100. Commit those to memory, and they will serve you well.

Now for the big payoff!

Do you remember when I asked you if you could remember the number:

**9229714843715122951901 12
1347407194172151394014938171 9205
97469015714909579019022163094620994**

Well, if you recall the test list at the beginning of this book under the link system, then you remember the number. If not, link the words below using the link system. Really try it. I think you will be absolutely amazed.

Again, the list was Banana, Picture Frame, Cat, Lightning Bolt, Post It Note, Mercury, Skateboard, Candle, Dime, Power Strip, Movie Ticket, Pencil, Poker Chip, Stool, Guitar, Baseball Cap, Stop Sign, Wind Chimes, Brush, Newspaper.

If you look at those words and convert them using the phonetic alphabet you will realize you have the number memorized!

BaNaNa (922), PiCTuRe FRaMe (9714 843), CaT (71), LighTNiNG BoLT (5122 951), PoST iT NoTe (901 1 21), MeRCuRy (3474), SKaTeBoaRD (071941), CaNDLe (7215), DiMe (13), PoweR STRiP (94 0149), MoVie TiCKeT (38171) , PeNCiL (9205), PoKeR CHiP (974 69), STooL (015), GuiTaR (714), BaSeBaLL CaP (9095 79), SToP SigN (019 02), wiND CHiMeS (21 630) BRuSH (946), NewSPaPeR (20994)

Congratulations! You just memorized a 90 digit number!!!

Now you know how to remember long strings of numbers.

Break the sequence into smaller groups of numbers, create words from those numbers, link those words together, and voila!

You've memorized that person's phone number without having to write it down. Comes in handy when you're out on the town, your phone is dead, and really, who carries pens anymore?

CRITIQUES

Many people say, "But I have my smart phone on me all the time, why should I put all this time into learning this complicated system that feels more like work than just remembering the information by itself?"

My answer: Sometimes your phone runs out of battery and you don't have anything to write with.

You never know when you'll need to exercise your memory.

Remembering someone's name is always in style.

Remembering a list forwards and backwards after hearing it once is a fun party stunt.

All the hard work is up front. Once you learn the system inside out, and become comfortable with its use, then you will find you effortlessly remember things that once would slip your mind. Every system is merely a method for cultivating the intent to pay attention to the information you want to store.

Mindfulness is a powerful ally.

CONCLUSION

Well! There you have it! Those are the memory systems that thousands of people have used for hundred of years to improve their memory before there was Google.

Now you, too, can increase your self reliance, and be confident in your day-to-day activities and not feel quite so worried when you forget your phone at home.

If you find yourself using any of these skills in your day-to-day life, I'd love to know how it's going for you. Success stories make my day!

THANKS

I would like to thank my parents for always supporting me in whatever peculiar interest I showed at the time while I was growing up. Who knew it would take me around the world!

Also, I would like to extend my heart-felt thanks to Banachek. A gentlemen among rogues who is the most kind and giving person I've had the pleasure to call friend. A world-class entertainer in his own right, and the person who did a lot of the heavy lifting for this book. If you ever have the chance to see him perform, run, don't walk, to the venue.

Finally, to Robert Yutzy, my high school debate teacher who introduced me to mnemonic systems and sparked my interest in demonstrations of accelerated memory.

ABOUT THE AUTHOR

Jonathan Pritchard is a Mentalist, speaker, author, and coach for people who want to achieve the impossible in life, business, and relationships.

He was born in California, raised in North Carolina, went to college in Kentucky, spent his summers in Ft. Lauderdale, and has since lived in Orlando FL, Austin TX, and Chicago IL.

Most days he wakes up without an alarm, practices kung fu, has coffee, reads for an hour, has lunch with a friend, runs some errands, talks with clients, and then you could probably find him watching a movie.

When not on the road speaking or performing, you can find him in Chicago working on his podcast, website, and other adventures.

Visit www.LikeAMindReader.com for more info.

www.ingramcontent.com/pod-product-compliance
Lightning Source LLC
Chambersburg PA
CBHW071634040426
42452CB00009B/1621